ANXIETY IN RELATIONSHIP

How to overcome anxiety, jealousy and negative thinking.

Dr. Marta Kaiser

© Copyright 2021 - All rights reserved.

The content contained within this book may not be reproduced, duplicated or transmitted without direct written permission from the author or the publisher.

Under no circumstances will any blame or legal responsibility be held against the publisher, or author, for any damages, reparation, or monetary loss due to the information contained within this book. Either directly or indirectly.

Legal Notice:

This book is copyright protected. This book is only for personal use. You cannot amend, distribute, sell, use, quote or paraphrase any part, or the content within this book, without the consent of the author or publisher.

Disclaimer Notice:

Please note the information contained within this document is for educational and entertainment purposes only. All effort has been executed to present accurate, up to date, and reliable, complete information. No warranties of any kind are declared or implied. Readers acknowledge that the author is not engaging in the rendering of legal, financial, medical or professional advice. The content within this book has been derived from various sources. Please consult a licensed professional before attempting any techniques outlined in this book.

By reading this document, the reader agrees that under no circumstances is the author responsible for any losses, direct or indirect, which are incurred as a result of the use of information contained within this document, including, but not limited to, — errors, omissions, or inaccuracies.

Introduction

Some theories propose that one cause of relational anxiety is an overly fearful attachment style. One theory states that overly fearful individuals are more prone to worry about threats in their relationships because they feel more out of control due to the inability to predict or understand them. Another theory is that dependent individuals have higher anxiety levels in relationships because they are more vulnerable to separations. Thus, when there is a threat of separation, they may feel the need to control their partner and stay in the relationship.

In cases where the anxiously attached individual feels that the relationship is not secure, they are likely to experience intense anxiety if things are not going well or if partners have any issues that threaten the relationship. This will cause them to feel overwhelmed by anxiety and may lead them to be clingy and possessive when their partner tries to leave.

This is also said to create a less fulfilling relationship because the partner with the anxious attachment style will be more likely to feel like they are being controlled in the relationship.

Relationship anxiety is generally thought to be a result of fear of losing or being left by a partner; however, the anxiety may also be about a partner controlling them or having unrealistic expectations of them.

The more anxious people are about their relationships, the higher their depression, loneliness, and isolation. They also tend to have smaller social networks. People who have strong relationships live longer than those same people who do not have strong relationships.

Obsessive Jealousy

Many relationships are victims of this danger called jealousy. That's why you must understand why you must deal with it and how.
Jealousy is a series of feelings accompanied by anger and unhappiness because someone or something you desire belongs to someone else. It can manifest as more than one emotion: resentment, disgust, anger, bitterness, helplessness, inadequacy, suspicion, hostility, and desperation. It's the fear that you may lose something or someone you consider indispensable to someone else.

A little measure of jealousy in a romantic relationship is natural, inevitable, and perhaps, healthy. You must have felt that sickening feeling in the pit of your stomach at least once in your life. However, while jealousy is quite natural to a certain degree, some people are dangerously jealous, and most often than not, their jealousy hurts their relationship. Yet again, some manifest irrational jealousy. This kind is unwarranted, baseless, and volatile. The person who manifests morbid jealousy lives in the continuous suspicion that the partner may be interested in a new and more interesting "object of love" able to replace them or take their place. The mind of the pathological jealous is invading with intrusive mental contents that, assuming the characteristics of obsession, absorb a considerable amount of time and energy.

Symptoms and How to Recognize Them

Jealousy has its symptoms, and a proper diagnosis will help you deal with it in the right way. Here are six signs that you are jealous, or that you have a jealous partner:

They Are Clingy

It's romantic when your partner always wants to be with you; this is bound to be the case in a new relationship. But when your partner insists on having you all to themselves, it's usually a bad sign. This is a red flag you want to look out for.

Jealousy doesn't look like jealousy in the beginning. It comes in the form of affection and attention overdose. It seems exciting, romantic, fun, and passionate. Your partner can't get enough of you. In the beginning, all these things are beautiful, but things will get ugly in the long term.

They Are Suspicious of You

If your partner questions your friendships, goes through your phone, wants details of your whereabouts, barges in unannounced and uninvited when you go out without them, you're in for some trouble. This sign of suspicion is an indication that your partner is jealous and doesn't trust you.

They Are Emotionally Dependent

It is a sign of extreme jealousy. People who are emotionally dependent remain in a relationship that makes them unhappy because they are scared of being alone. Such partners don't value themselves. They derive their sense of self from their partner; this makes them feel easily threatened. They become jealous in no time and are always in need of reassurance. A sign of emotional dependency is a willingness to accept outrageous conditions in exchange for acceptance and love.

They Try to Control Your Life

Jealousy causes partners to have unhealthy and scary controlling behaviors. If they want to regulate your calls, friendships, and how you relate with others, it's time to call time out and have a serious conversation. Address it properly and you'll kill jealousy before it ruins your relationship.

They're Always Around

A sign that your partner is green with jealousy is when they start following you around and neglecting their activities and interests to keep an eye on you. Sure, this can be a sincere desire to be with you. It would be best if you were cautious when your partner abandons things in their life, they couldn't do without spending unnecessary time with you.

They Suddenly Hate Your Favorite Things

Certainly, when your partner insists you stay away from people, they see a sexual threat, a clear sign of jealousy. When they disapprove of people, places, things you love, collectively, then all the sirens are blaring. This is a major sign of jealousy in a relationship. Such people don't want you to get better or be happy without them; they feel threatened if you find fulfillment in something else.

Dealing with Jealousy

Jealousy drains a relationship of essential ingredients such as unconditional love, compassion, trust, vulnerability, freedom, and much more. It creates tension, suspicion, sadness, and bitterness. When it creeps into your love life, you need to deal with it and make your relationship healthy again. Here are some ways you can successfully overcome jealousy:

Acknowledge It

It's natural to feel ashamed about being jealous, but don't deny or ignore it. You can't neglect a wound and expect to heal; you'll have to get immediate medical attention. Likewise, you need to be honest about your feelings and acknowledge your jealousy before you can heal. Begin with acknowledging how your insecurities make you feel and how they are damaging your relationship.

Use Your Jealousy as an Opportunity

Feelings of jealousy are stirred up because of a relationship problem, either from you or your partner. So, you need to look at the jealous behavior you're portraying and ask what that jealousy is attempting to solve. For instance, if jealousy springs up because your partner broke your trust in the past and created an opportunity for doubt to creep in, your jealousy is not the problem. Instead, your partner's breach of trust is the real problem. Moreover, if you're taking out your insecurity on your partner, then insecurity is the problem.

You need to look at your jealousy as an opportunity to solve a problem.

Focus on making sure you and your partner have no reason to be jealous.

Discover Your Insecurities

If you've noticed that you are overly jealous, you need to discover the cause and deal with it. How do you do this? Ninety percent of the time, jealousy springs from insecurities, so make a list of them. Do you look down on yourself? Do you wonder why your partner is still with you? Do you continuously feel other people are better than you? When you do this, you'll gain control over how you respond to these weaknesses and start working on them.

Work on Your Self-Esteem

After discovering your insecurities and making a list of the feelings fueling your jealousy, prescribe a solution for each of them. You might discover that you've been comparing yourself to your partner's ex and have been feeling inadequate. To remedy this, write down all your good qualities and everything your partner loves about you. Do the same for every insecurity; afterward, isolate yourself from anything that makes you feel inferior.

Find the Cause of the Problem

Is your insecurity or jealousy caused by unhealed wounds from your past? Some people struggle with jealousy because of the traumatic childhood experience they had. Others might be insecure because of a defect or an addiction. No matter what it is, get to the root of that feeling of jealousy, and get professional help to enable you to deal with the toxic feelings for good.

Open Up About It

Often, partners detect jealousy way before the other person says anything. But the ideal way to deal with it is to communicate effectively and open up about it to your partner. The truth is, even though insecurities are playing a role, your partner might be making you jealous either knowingly or unknowingly. Through effective communication and a great deal of honesty, you can take responsibility for causing the relationship problem. At the same time, your partner will become more aware of their role in fueling your jealousy and will make necessary adjustments. This way, your partner helps you deal with any feelings of jealousy—given that they are genuine and are not cheating on you.

Learn Healthy Patterns for Coping

Jealousy can become a bad habit and destroy your relationship, especially when the feelings spring from insecurities. This means you'll need to learn healthy coping patterns. Come to terms with seeing your partner with members of the opposite sex that seem better than you. Accept that you'll need to learn to trust your partner over obsessive thoughts and paranoid feelings of infidelity. Declare war against jealousy and replace it with selflove and care. Get busy, prioritize physical fitness, nurture your emotional and mental health, and chase your dreams.

How to Help Your Partner Overcome Jealousy

Now that you know the signs to look out to know if your partner is jealous, you need to know how to help them. Yes, you need to help them overcome that jealousy, and doing so will strengthen your relationship.

If your partner tells you about their jealousy, the most bizarre thing to do is defend yourself. Don't say you're not at fault. Don't call them paranoid. Don't feel hurt that they don't trust you. Above all, don't laugh in their face and play down their concerns. Think about it. A jealous person feels that a special relationship is threatened; scolding or criticizing them will only worsen things.

Show Acceptance

Even though you might dislike your partner's feelings, you must know how best to respond to them. The best way is to accept that they feel that way and that you need to help them overcome it. Ensure you don't appear disappointed and avoid making them feel guilty for a feeling they can't control. Show acceptance and affirm that their feelings are worth investigating.

Understand Their Pain

You might see anxiety, anger, and other emotions manifesting due to jealousy. Yet you need to know the pain your partner is going through because they love you and can't stand to lose you. Listen to the pain and show them you're there to provide support.

Be Compassionate

What a jealous person needs most of the time is reassurance. So be compassionate and show your partner that you care. You care about their feelings, and you want to make them feel better.

Be Conscious of Triggers

Jealous people have triggers that set off these emotions. For some, it is listening to you talk about your ex, seeing you with attractive people, etc. Reassure your partner that you understand their triggers, and you'd do your best to help them avoid these things.

Get Your Act Together

Sincerely ask yourself, "What am I doing to make my partner jealous?" If your partner doesn't trust you, it's probably for a reason; discover it. Also, decide to make amends by giving up certain lifestyles or behaviors to help your partner trust you more. Do you still have dinner with your ex? Do you talk about finding other people attractive? Are you transparent and honest about your relationships and activities? Be willing to change something to boost your partner's confidence in you.

Come to an Agreement

Have a conversation with your partner and agree on changes that will remove jealousy from your relationship for good. Share your expectations in the relationship and what needs to be done to build trust and intimacy.

Although you want to trust and unconditional love in your relationship, do not ignore jealousy. Neither ignore nor embrace it. Instead, join forces with your partner and deal with it. Use it as an excuse to evolve in your love life and form a stronger bond with your partner. Make jealousy the reason you became a better version of yourself. Confident, courageous, aware of your self-worth, and successful.

Fear of Abandonment

People close to you are an important part of your life, and you fear that they may desert you. It's hard to avoid becoming anxious if you think you might be abandoned. This could be because of a long-term traumatic event you experienced as a child or due to an uncomfortable or harmful connection you have as an adult. It is nearly impossible to have healthy relationships if you are afraid of abandonment. This paralyzing fear can keep you from engaging with others and may even lead you to build a fortress around yourself to keep yourself safe. You could also be sabotaging your relationships on purpose.

According to experts, fear of abandonment emerges because people encounter disruptions in the normal developmental process of various cognitive and emotional skills and difficulties with former relationships. The fear of abandonment is, by most measures, one of the most common and devastating fears to many people. Fearing desertion may cause people to act and think in a way that negatively impacts their relationships.

In the long run, non-adaptive dealing with their fear of abandonment can result in them being abandoned. A result of this worry is that it can be rather harmful. One of the first steps to addressing abandonment fears is to understand them.

On the other hand, abandonment difficulties create a constant worry of losing what is important to them. They are also likely to demonstrate behaviors that coerce others out of the position, leaving them unprepared for the losses.

Extreme Fear of Being Abandoned in Relationships

Adults who did not grow up in households where they were abandoned may still experience abandonment-related sentiments. Relationship losses can include the death of a loved one, as well as separation or divorce. Additionally, children or adults may be abandoned. Regardless of the method is employed, the outcome can be far-reaching. The connection this relationship has on a person's relationships whether intimate, social, or professional, may cause complications for any additional relationships a person forms.

An otherwise healthy relationship can be affected by a fear of desertion. It is common for partners to wonder if their partner is having an affair. In this way, prior relationships with other people can induce feelings of worry. Previous loss or anxiety concerns could also contribute to it. Work to keep your partner from leaving may be a strategy for people who are terrified of being abandoned. Relationships may require a great deal of effort on both parties' parts. Next, the relationship can tend to crumble since their partner never appreciates or reciprocates their efforts.

You may be afraid that someone you care about will physically leave and never return. You may be afraid that someone may disregard your emotional requirements. Both can be detrimental to your relationships with a parent, a partner, or a friend.

While psychological abandonment is less visible than physical abandonment, it is no less distressing. Each of us has emotional needs. When those needs are not addressed, you may experience feelings of unworthiness, not being loved, and disconnection. As a result, you can feel extremely alone, even if you are physically present in a relationship. If you've ever been the victim of emotional abandonment, particularly as a child, you may live in constant terror that it may happen again.

Anxiety over Abandonment in Partnerships

You may be fearful about exposing yourself to a relationship. You may struggle with trust and obsess over your connection.

This may cause you to become distrustful about your relationship. Your fears may eventually compel the other person to withdraw, repeating the cycle.

Signs

Millions of people are afflicted with terror. When it comes to relationships, the behaviors that may emerge from fear of abandonment include the following:

- Having difficulty trusting others
- Struggles with being inflexible and nitpicky
- Rapid attachment to even absent partners or relationships
- Attempting to stifle emotions. You're aware that your insecurity is driving your lover away, but you cannot locate the magic dial that would turn down the fear
- Leaving fast to avoid becoming too connected
- Inability to commit totally and having had only a few long-term partnerships
- Desire to please
- Attempting to coerce your partner into doing something that will make you feel safer. This adds

strain to the connection and decreases its mutuality quotient

- A sense of insecurity and unworthiness of love

- Suffer from severe separation anxiety

- A penchant for overthinking situations and exerting considerable effort to deduce hidden meanings

- Managing repressed emotions and difficulties of
- control Twisting yourself into a pretzel to conceal your fear. You lose your authenticity in the process of attempting to save the relationship

- Maintaining ties regardless of how harmful they are
-
- Difficulty with emotional intimacy
-
- You are frequently envious of everyone you meet

- Creating an emotional bond between you and your companion. This produces a horrible scenario in which you rely on them more than they rely on you. As the chasm grows wider, your desperation grows stronger, perpetuating a terrible cycle

- Suffering from generalized anxiety and despair

- Are extremely receptive to criticism

Constantly overanalyze the relationship, frequently focusing on the faults or problems rather than on the great characteristics of their partner and connection

- Will pursue connections with emotionally unavailable individuals

- Frequent self-blame

- Having unreasonable expectations of your relationship, desiring excessively early. You overreact and over-need, which diminishes your sense of self-worth and your partner's sense of self-worth

- Jealousy over their partner's work relations

- Being unfaithful to their spouse or partner

Symptoms

Many of the behaviors associated with abandonment anxieties are shared by those who dread abandonment. However, some are more prevalent than others. Among these symptoms are the following:

Revolving Around Relationships

Certain individuals may engage in several superficial partnerships. They may be afraid of closeness and look for an excuse to exit a relationship before the other person does.

Attempting to Sabotage Relationships

Certain individuals may behave irrationally to get out of partnerships. For instance, you may purposefully push away a partner to avoid feeling upset if they depart.

Adherence to Toxic Relationships

Certain individuals suffering from abandonment issues may remain in relationships despite a desire to depart. The fear of being alone is more potent.

Constant Need for Reassurance

Certain individuals may be perpetually on the lookout for a buddy or relationship and may demand emotional promises. They may frequently encourage friends or lovers to make broad declarations like "I'll always be here" and then claim they're lying.

Effects on Relationship

Fear of abandonment is particularly individual. Certain individuals are fearful primarily of losing a romantic companion. Others are afraid of being abandoned in other relationships. To illustrate how persons who fear abandonment might negotiate a relationship, consider how a traditional relationship might begin and progress. This is particularly true for sexual relationships, but intimate friendships share many parallels as well.

Meeting and Becoming Familiar with One Another

You feel relatively secure at this time. You have not yet developed an emotional attachment to the other person. As a result, you continue living your life while spending time with your chosen individual.

Honeymoon Period

This phase begins when you decide to commit. You're inclined to overlook any yellow or red flags simply because you are friends. You begin spending excessive time with the other person, and you always have a good time. You begin to experience a sense of security.

Practical Relationship

The honeymoon period cannot last indefinitely. Whatever the degree to which two individuals get along, life always intervenes. People become ill, have family issues, begin working long hours, worry about money, and require time to complete tasks.

While this is a perfectly natural and desirable development in a relationship, it can be frightening for those who fear abandonment as they may interpret it as an indication that the other person is withdrawing. If you have this worry, you are probably struggling with yourself and avoiding expressing your concerns out of fear of appearing needy.

The Minor

Human beings are fallible. They have moods and concerns. Regardless matter how much they feel about another person, they cannot and should not be expected to put that person first constantly. It is unavoidable that an apparent slight will occur, even more so once the honeymoon period has passed. This is frequently expressed through an unreturned text message, an unanswered phone call, or a desire for a few days of solitude.

The Outcome

This is a watershed moment for people who dread abandonment. If you experience this worry, you are almost certainly convinced that your partner has lost interest in you. What follows is almost entirely controlled by the severity of the fear of abandonment and the sufferer's preferred coping technique.

Certain individuals respond to this by becoming clinging and demanding, requiring their partners to demonstrate their love by leaping through hoops. Others flee, rejecting their lovers before being rejected themselves. Others believe it is their fault for the slight and seek to make themselves into the "ideal mate" to prevent the other person from leaving.

In actuality, the affront is almost certainly not an insult at all. Said, people occasionally act in ways that their relationships do not understand. In a good relationship, the partner may identify the circumstance for a natural reaction unrelated to the relationship. Or they may be offended by it yet address it calmly or with a quick argument. In either case, a single perceived slight does not exert a disproportionate amount of impact on the partner's emotions.

A person who has been abandoned may be more prone to developing longterm mental health problems. These are frequently motivated by a fear of recurrence of abandonment. Later in life, a child abandoned by a primary caregiver or parent may have panic attacks or hostility. These actions might cause potential close partners and friends to become estranged. Lack of parental care can also affect a child's self-esteem.

Fears of abandonment can hinder an individual's ability to trust others. They may make it more difficult for an individual to feel worthy or intimate. These worries may predispose an individual to anxiety, sadness, codependence, or other problems. Issues of abandonment are often associated with borderline personality disorder (BPD) and attachment anxiety. Someone who experiences low self-esteem due to childhood abandonment may seek out connections that validate their thoughts.

If your fear is low and well-controlled, you may be able to overcome it simply by increasing your awareness of your inclinations and developing new behavioral tactics. However, for most people fear of abandonment is rooted in deep-seated concerns that are difficult to resolve on their own. Therefore, professional counseling is frequently necessary to overcome this anxiety and permanently alter your ideas and behaviors.

Surround yourself with like-minded whatever stage of life you are currently in. Compile a list of your present interests, passions, and aspirations. Then connect with others who share your passions.

How to Overcome the Fear of Abandonment

he first step in living with someone is to put out their fear of T abandonment. Saying it is far easier than doing it. This has to be done, though. Within you and your relationships, you have to build up your trust. You must know that you are caring and worthy of love. You must understand that.

You must learn how to realize, by enhancing your self-esteem, that you deserve love and to find someone deserving of your affection. Perhaps you can't do it all on your own. Can I cope in a relationship with abandonment issues? Continuing healing starts with awareness. Everything begins with what you see in yourself, how you view love and marriage, and whether you are willing to have more stable relationships and personal emotional wellbeing.

Do you know your triggers? These stimuli can be involuntary at first, but you become very aware of them as you start the process of healing. An event or spoken word is a trigger that sends the past emotion that causes you to think and feel those thoughts. Such thoughts and feelings produce a continuum of actions that can be defensive or self-sabotage mechanisms.

When you understand these stimuli, you will pause from a clear perspective to analyze your thoughts and emotions. This helps you to respond with a conscious mental filter rather than emotional. It is a reality, but we don't always feel our feelings. The more you use this process in your recovery, the more symptoms will be eradicated. It's not fear of giving up; it's how we treat it and undermine our ties. It can conflict with or improve our relationships. Once we can deal with this simple fear, we have access to its healing qualities.

This anxiety is caused by feeling drawn to someone. Most people complain about their loss in a prison of their own making: "I am too weak, too afraid to be in a relationship."

Identify What Isn't Working

- You want so much so fast and have unreasonable aspirations for your partner. You respond over and

over, making you and your partner feel less for you
and yourself

- You're aware that your anxiety pushes your partner
  away, but you can't find the ability to turn fear away
- Trying to influence your mate to make it better for
  you. It raises strain and reduces the quotient of the
  partnership
- Try to hide the emotional cups as rage or
  covetousness. The vacuum cups specifically target the
  partner irrespective of how you play them and are
  heard by your partner's special radar
- Twisting yourself up to cover your fear. You lose
  your credibility in trying to save the relationship
- Letting your partner feel responsible for you
  emotionally. It generates the negative situation that
  you need them more than they need you. This can
  lead to depression worsening, and a catastrophic
  loop is created
- You loathe when you fear that your partner is causing

  insecurity

What to Do

- Avoid beating yourself. It is accidental to fear abandonment. You didn't do it. You didn't sign up for anything. It's not your fault
- Consider this fear as part of being a human being. Give yourself unconditional self-love and compassion rather than judging yourself as "weak"
- Choose to stop putting your fear at the feet of your partner (or anyone else)
- Instead of asking your partner to "fix," take 100 percent responsibility when your anxiety erupts
- Let us use the fear of abandonment to build emotional selfconfidence
- Bring your partner for yourself with self-confidence

- Be personally interested in the deconstruction of abandonment. The tools can help you handle your own emotional needs structured, not necessarily to rely on your partner
- Remember the fact that no one other than you are responsible for making you feel safe. When you look for the answer in your partner, you give away your power

- Leap personal-self-assurance but do it on your own. This is not all that we achieve. This is a long, steady, and intermittent path to emotional self-assurance

- Only turn if you find yourself looking for reassurance again to your partner! Get back on the path! Make yourself 100 percent responsible

- Transforming abandonment anxiety into emotional autonomy implies that you embrace your separateness as an individual. It helps you stop your partner's vulnerability and take responsibility for your emotional needs

Some Tips for Overcoming Abandonment Issues

Let Someone In

Big changes begin with small steps. Teach yourself to trust again—don't worry; this does not have to be serious! Trust in people does not necessarily mean revealing your darkest, deepest secrets. Begin by telling friends small things they don't know about your life. You will improve your connections by sharing knowledge and knowing that people are interested and involved in your life. Over time, you will share more critical stuff that you don't find as frightening as you once did. By engaging yourself in sharing, you can think more about people and not always feel so worried.

Confidence is a big step forward in any relationship, from close family members to good friends to the person with whom you are existing. If you feel troublesome at first, this is natural, do not judge yourself! Go at a pace appropriate for you and spend time knowing that no one will deceive you.

Find an Outlet

Seek a comfortable place where you can share your apprehension and anxiety. You do not have to allocate this with anybody; you can write a diary or set up a blog protected by a password, which helps you write freely without fear of judgment. Writing down the information also allows us to make things simpler and is an excellent way to do it all. Journals are a fantastic place to continue if you are still finding it difficult to talk with people about your personal life.

If you feel more comfortable singing or constructing works of art, go for it. You don't have to share that you do it (if you don't want to); keep it for yourself. Songwriting is a beautiful way to share emotions, and songs from others help us understand how we feel. The concept of being part of a team that has to invest in others can be the right choice too. A sense of community and appreciation can be a pleasant remembrance of people.

Be Responsible for Your Feelings

Part of working on your mind and all the related stuff (self-confidence, problems of intimacy, and worry) is what you hear. It could be easy to hide in the safety of denial and not admit that something feels scary or upsetting; while it feels good in the short term, it does not help.

Depression in Your Life

Depression should not be confused with demoralization or sadness, which we can all experience. Some people may experience a change of mood, especially feeling angry and isolated. You may have come across an individual with stress. Think of how that person usually behaves. Such people are emotional and upset.

You cannot even establish the real cause of their sorrow, but they mostly attribute the causes of many weird episodes to their lives. At that moment, you can wonder what to do as therapy for them. However, it is good to visit a physician if you find your relative suffering from that menace. Such disorder is generally referred to as depression.

Depression can primarily be associated with stress and sadness; however, it is a broader concept. Some scientist defines this disorder as the long-term effect of experiencing anxiety and grief. Yes, it is accurate, but depression is not stress or sadness in some other instances. Take an example of the emotional reaction you feel after seeing your beloved or relative dead. Then it would be exceptional distress or sorrow.

Overcoming Depression

Depression is a common yet often misunderstood condition in today's society that anyone can experience at any time. In many cases, depression may be temporary and only last for a few weeks or months, but long-term or chronic depression may require professional help to resolve.

Experts in the mental health field agree that it is unnecessary to have a mental illness to be depressed. Many people experience mild cases of depression without ever having sought to help from a professional.

Depression is not always considered to be the same as being sad, but rather an emotional state where one feels sad and hopeless for no apparent reason, often keeping them in bed all day. One may feel irritable and unable to get anything done because of the overwhelming sadness that they are feeling.

Through Diet

Giving your brain certain nutrients can help you improve your attitude. According to Dr. Barish-Wreden, depression can improve by up to 60 percent with proper nutrition! With all the nutrients you need, your brain has the fuel it needs to have clarity and be more resilient to mental illness and stress. The American Dietetic Association says that eating habits are often impacted by mental illness, which then causes nutritional imbalances that make it even harder to improve your condition once you have it. Therefore, a good diet is a preventative measure, but it also impacts your ability to get better.

If your body doesn't have the nutrients it needs to run your vital systems, it starts to cut corners and become inefficient. Essential functions will be impaired and unable to run at optimal capacity. An unbalanced diet makes you wearier and deficient in critical vitamins and minerals, which are both factors that can reduce your mental health outcomes. Additionally, nutritional imbalances can interfere with your hormone levels, triggering stress, depression, and anxiety.

Eating a balanced diet can make a profound change in your mental state, and a balanced diet starts with macronutrients such as carbs, proteins, and fats. You'll want to include a balance of these foods in your diet unless your doctor tells you otherwise because they each play an essential role in your brain.

Our diet culture often conveys the idea that carbs are bad, and that's not the case. Your brain needs carbs to function. You should reach for complex carbs such as brown rice and other whole grains, rather than simple carbs like sugar or white bread. Whole grains do not eliminate nutritional parts of the grain in the processing process, so they have additional nutrients like fiber, which keep you balanced.

Fats in your diet are also important. They are another type of food that people are taught is "bad." Fats help protect your organs, and they serve as energy stores between meals and keep you insulated. Nevertheless, some fats are more nutritionally dense than others. You will want to limit trans and unsaturated fats because they can harm your health. Some fats are vital, though.

Omega-3 fatty acids, for example, found in fish like salmon, promote brain clarity, and omega-6 fatty acids, found in vegetable oils, are also known for improving mood conditions. Finally, monosaturated fats are healthy fats that can improve your overall health, and they can be found in sources like olive oil and avocados.

Proteins, found mostly in meat, eggs, dairy, and soy, are a building block for your body, and they allow you to repair tissues and build muscles. They have a varied and vital role in your body, and it's important to note that you'll want to eat these foods several times throughout the day because your body does not store them, so you use them as you eat them, which is why eating three meals a day is helpful.

Be careful of sugar. While there's not a problem with sugar in moderation, too much sugar can cause bodily inflammation. This inflammation can then result in depression and anxiety. Sugar is often something people reach for when they feel sad or stressed, so it can contribute to you struggling to have the nutritional balance you need to get better.

Stop Being Catastrophic

It helps to remember that thought patterns that were healthy can become stale and turn toxic at one point in your life. As you learn and have new needs and wants, you also must learn to change your thinking. Just like you probably enjoy rearranging your house every so often, it's also nice to assess and refresh your thought patterns every so often. You were not the same person you were ten years ago, and you won't be the same person ten years from now, so what provides fulfillment now may fill you with dread in the future. Change is how you grow, so learn to move with it rather than trying to resist it.

Do Not Constantly Brood Negative Thoughts

Be careful not to shift your negative thinking towards new negative ways of thinking. Finding positive outlooks to shape your worldview will help you resist mental conditions and stress. When negativity strikes, play devil's advocate and try to figure out how that negativity is false.

The famous quote, "If you want different results, you have to do things differently," is so profound. When you feel stuck or restless, all you have to do is to choose to act differently. What you're doing isn't working, so it cannot hurt to try acting in a way that you wouldn't normally. Challenge yourself to think in new ways.

Start to affirm "I want to" rather than "I have to." Otherwise, when you have to do something, it will feel like a chore. Wanting to do something is more enthusiastic, and it helps you choose options that reflect what you want to accomplish rather than what you feel pressured to complete.

If you have trouble breaking through the negativity, start with a small change in your view. For example, if you keep thinking, "I am worthless," start to think about just one thing that gives you worth and say, "I do have worth." Then, whenever you catch yourself thinking that you are worthless, you can start to correct that thought process and build up to more fully recognizing ways that you do have worth. When things go wrong, find a silver lining.

Keep assessing yourself to make sure your thought patterns aren't turning against you. When you lose awareness, that's when the stress, depression, and anxiety sneak into your life.

New perspectives become old, so learn to identify when that is the case for you.

Focus on the Good Things

While there are people who will experience depression no matter how much happiness they try to surround themselves with, it is important to focus on the good things in one's life to help keep depression at bay.

While negative feelings may seem to overwhelm a person stuck in a cycle of an everlasting depression, it is important not to let those feelings dictate one's entire life or ability to live a happy and fulfilling existence.

One of the greatest ways to keep depression at bay is to surround oneself with friends and family members who are happy, embrace a loving relationship with another person, find goals one is passionate about and thrive to achieve them.

Always remind oneself of the many beautiful things in life that make up for the intense sadness one may feel during periods of depression. One should seek beauty in nature, art, and other entertainment forms such as movies, plays, and music.

People who receive treatment for depression often find that if they can manage to focus on the positive things in their life, it will help them get through those times when they feel overwhelmed and unable to function properly.

Be Kind to Yourself

If you are working all the time and constantly running around trying to get certain tasks done, you're going to be prone to stress and other mental dysfunctions, so you need to take care of yourself and find time for relaxation. Self-care is about calming down and investing time in yourself. It's doing anything that you feel you are lacking but would like to do.

Recognize that there's nothing wrong with needing to be alone sometimes and treating yourself every once in a while. It doesn't make you selfish to focus on yourself for a little time each day. You need that time to reorient your brain and recover from the daily stresses of your life.

The following are some tips to help with your journey:

- Make time for recreation. While many people neglect their needs, you do need this time.

  During recreational times, you can do activities that you do because you love them

- Have a spa day, so you can relax and escape the intensity of your life
- Keep a journal to reflect on how you feel
- If you are extroverted, spend extra time around other people, and if you're introverted, take some spare time on your own during recreational hours
- Stay in touch with your emotional and physical needs
- Keep your treatment needs organized (using a calendar or other planning systems) to ensure you take medications and attend sessions or appointments that will keep you in top shape
- Treat yourself to nice things every once in a while. It always feels rewarding to save up and have something special that we wouldn't usually get
- Take time away from technology because technology can cause sleep problems and distract you from your needs

Living the Present

One important aspect of maintaining a happy and healthy lifestyle is learning to live in the present moment and not let the past or future dictate how one feels at any given time.

Many people who are stuck in depression mode focus on things that happened in their pasts or may even be worrying about their futures, which can cause them to miss out on opportunities for joy right now.

It is important to learn to enjoy every day and embrace life as it comes. If a person can focus on the present moment and live their lives daily, it will be much easier to stay out of depression in the future.

Do Not Lose Connection with Others

When you have trouble breaking from your limiting perspective, you can get feedback from other people because then you have more information that you can use to readjust your perspective. Considering other's views on a problem helps you see beyond your blind spots, and it teaches you that there is another one you can find for every perspective you have.

A support system is a vital part of your mental health. A 2015 survey showed that people with a support system willing to help them emotionally had a decreased average stress level. A support system gives you people who will listen to your problems and allow you to express your emotional state. It prevents social isolation, which is a known factor that makes people more at risk for mental illness. Mental Health First Aid suggests that a sound support system has anywhere from one to ten people representing various parts of your life (work, family, hobbies, etc.).

Exercises for Defeating Anxiety

Defeating anxiety at the moment will also be a major tool that you need to have when it comes to navigating a relationship with anxiety. Anxiety is something that will plague just about anyone at some point. When you don't know how to manage your anxiety, you can allow it to run rampant and destroy anything that you are attempting to do. It could be your way of getting control of your feelings, so they do not continue to be a problem as well. No matter the method, however, it is important that you have your coping mechanisms for anxiety, below will be addressed a few of them.

Physical Activity

The most recommended, as well as simple and affordable for anyone, is physical activity. It is easy to integrate into everyone's life, and also exercise is just as powerful as most of the medications to combat anxiety.

Grounding Exercise

The first exercise that you are going to be introduced to is the exercise to ground yourself. This one is especially useful if you currently feel like you are too stressed out or like you are losing control. When the emotions are getting the best of you, the sooner you can get them back under your control, the better. The sooner you can control those emotions, the sooner you will ensure that you are actively making it a point to keep yourself under control. The sooner you can do that, the better you will do in the long run with your anxiety.

Many people will use it to get their anxiety under control at the moment through this grounding exercise. This is designed to help you stop yourself at the moment so you can shift your brain from that irrational emotional response back into a more positive, rational, and logical state of activation. You will do this by essentially forcing yourself to shift your thought processes over, and one way to do so is through grounding exercises.

This particular grounding exercise will have you engage as many of your senses as possible to stop yourself and engage in that positive thinking pattern that you will need.

To begin, you will follow these steps:

1. Breathe deeply through your nose and hold for a few seconds. You want the breath to be slow as you inhale and then slowly exhale it out of your mouth. Repeat this a few times. Deep breathing will help your body to calm down.

2. Look around you. Now identify five things that you can find all around you. They should be five things that you can actively see. Describe them to yourself as detailed as you can. Perhaps you see that the apple on the table next to you is perfectly smooth and round and that the skin is mottled with tiny freckles across it, but it is shiny, and it has a perfect stem attached to it. Describe each of the five things in that much detail to yourself.

3. When you have finished looking at five things, you must now stop, breathe again, and listen closely. You must now identify four things that you can hear all

around you. What are they? How do they sound? What is the pitch? The tempo? Is it reverberating? Is it whiny? Label it as well as you can.

4. Take a deep breath. Then, you must find three things that you can touch. Run your fingers or your feet over them. Focus on the textures, sensations, and temperatures. You want to identify as much as you can about the feeling.

5. Take another deep breath in and out. Then, smell the air. What can you smell around you? Perhaps you can still smell the faint, slightly floral scent of your deodorant or the food cooked in the other room. Name it and describe it. Is it pungent? Floral? Sweet? Sickly-sweet? Bitter? Smelly? Go through the process with two distinct smells that you can identify around you.

6. Finally, you will take another deep breath and name the feeling you have right that moment. What is it that you feel? Put a name on it and recognize that it is okay to feel that way.

When you name the feeling that you have, you can take control of it. Even better, as you go through this entire process, you are essentially working hard to ensure that you know what you feel so you can defeat those feelings at the end of the day.

Visualization Exercise

Another great exercise to help defeat anxiety in its tracks is the visualization exercise. This will essentially have you stop, recognize that you are anxious, and then visualize something that will help to alleviate that anxiety from you. It draws from many different meditation principles and practices and is designed to help you feel complete and utter control of yourself and how you are feeling.

It helps you distance yourself, so to speak—you can put that barrier between yourself and those feelings so you can then defeat them entirely to help yourself. If you can master this, you will know that you can manage your emotions properly. You will be able to properly see how you can calm down, all by stopping to imagine them in the first place.

You must first set up a sort of paradise for yourself in your mind. What do you want to see? Imagine the most beautiful, calming setting that you can and allow yourself to go there. You want to bring yourself to that point so you can defeat the anxiety. Perhaps, you visualize yourself on the beach. Maybe you stop and consider how your sand feels. You imagine the feeling of beach sand on your feet—the sun on your shoulders and your head. You hear the sounds of the water rushing against the shore.

This process is designed to help you recognize just how likely you are to process everything. After you paint the image in your mind that you will revisit every time you feel stressed out, you will then work to ensure that you can recall it at will. You will essentially be coming up with a way in which, no matter how you feel, you can stop, identify it, and relate to it. You will see that you will be able to distance yourself from the feelings of anxiety when they arise, allowing you to reclaim and reengage with that positive, logical side of your brain to make use of that instead.

Mindfulness Exercise

One last exercise that you can do to help tame anxiety at the moment is a mindfulness exercise. Mindfulness is the act of stopping yourself and feeling any emotions that you may need to feel in the moment. It recognizes that you can disengage from those feelings to figure out what you will need to do to begin to distance yourself from them. Essentially, you will learn how to overcome those negative emotions once and for all to know what you are doing.

Mindfulness is a meditation that involves utter awareness. You are focusing on labeling everything that you can as much as you can to see how you can properly process everything. It is the idea that ultimately, you will be able to actively work to feel those feelings without letting them rule over you.

To begin, you must first be able to focus without distraction. You should find somewhere that is perfectly quiet at first, and you should get comfortable where you are.

Then, follow these simple steps:

1. Take a deep breath in and out. Repeat this for a minute until you start to feel calmer.

2. Quietly stop and focus on your thoughts. How are you feeling? Why are you feeling that way?

3. Let your thoughts come and go without stopping or interacting with them. Let them pass you by. Imagine that they are leaves floating gently and lazily down a

stream, one by one, coming and going without any intervention.

4. Remain in this state and breathe quietly and deeply until you feel better. When you notice that your mind wanders, return it to the topic you consider and move on.

Discuss with Your Partner about Each Other's Needs

Any good partnership relies on effective communication. Failure to communicate properly can result in misunderstandings, damaged feelings, and a variety of other problems. Mindful communication is being more aware of how you connect with others regularly.

When the other person speaks to you, it all boils down to being present. This is especially important in a relationship. Your partner needs you to be present, and they want to see that you can listen to and understand their thoughts and feelings. However, real communication has become increasingly difficult these days.

People are more comfortable texting each other or using social media than having actual face-to-face conversations. No matter where you look, people look down at their phones instead of facing the person sitting next to them. It doesn't matter if it's on a date or if the person is sitting right next to you at home. Think about it. How frequently do you communicate with your partner?

- Take some time to notice if you do any of the following things:

- Forming responses before your partner finishes their sentence

- Thinking of something else, even when your partner is talking to you

- Feeling impatient during a conversation

- Cutting your partner short when they speak

- Thinking about your own experience when it relates to something that happened to your partner

- Feeling bored when you have to deliberate something or have an honest conversation

These are some of the common communication patterns that have developed between people today. All of it harms your life and your relationship with your partner. This is where mindful communication comes to the rescue. Whether you want to improve your relationship with your partner or work on your social skills in general, mindfulness adds the necessary dimension to successful communication.

Committing to mindful communication with your partner means you will be committing to the following:

- Listening to your partner without being distracted

- Holding a conversation without being too emotional

- Being non-judgmental when you talk, fight, or argue with your partner

- Accepting partner's perspective, even if it is different from yours

- Validating yourself and your partner

All of these are important and will benefit your relationship in so many ways.

As you know, communication is particularly important when it comes to romantic relationships. Being able to deliberate all issues freely, make plans, and set goals for the future are vital for a successful relationship. Otherwise, how could two partners handle their responsibilities, challenges, and expectations?

However, what happens if one of you is suffering from anxiety? Of course, it depends on how severe the anxiety is. Even so, no matter its level of development, the personal connection will be in some way affected.

You or your partner might encounter difficulties reacting in a healthy way when either of you expresses an opinion or an emotion. For instance, it is common to misread someone's intent or misinterpret the meaning of individual conversations. Anxiety works in many ways as a filter. When it clouds your vision, you might act in a way that will eventually damage your relationship. Any joke, comment, or harmless critique can lead to an overreaction that will strain any couple, even more than the anxiety itself.

You should take a break and figure out what warranted such a negative reaction or outburst. Your partner may be suffering from a form of anxiety, and they are overwhelmed by the strain. If you are the one with this problem, you need to acknowledge what's wrong and express it. If you don't, your partner will think you're cruel or aggressive for no reason, or that they are the problem.

Relationship Communication Anxiety

Anxiety has a severe emotional effect on people. The partner is always affected in some way due to seeing their significant other suffering and going through a life-crippling experience. In many cases, the one suffering from anxiety will suppress emotions or feelings. Emotions carry a great deal of power, and some people find it too challenging to face them. Those afraid to express themselves emotionally have likely lived in a household where this behavior was discouraged.

The act of suppressing emotions is a sign that the person is trying to hold onto a semblance of control. If you find yourself behaving this way, it might be because you are scared of losing that control and allowing the locked-up feelings to overwhelm you. Naturally, the biggest issue here is when it comes to negative emotions, as they have such a substantial impact on a person's life.

You might think that if you let it all out, you will change your partner's feelings, and whatever good opinions and thoughts they have about you will be gone, causing damage to the relationship. However, while you may think of this as a solution, it leads to even more problems. Acting this way will increase the amount of anxiety you experience. You will find less peace of mind until one day when it will all come out in a wild burst. It's difficult to suppress those feelings forever, and when they come to the surface, they will cloud all judgment.

Communication anxiety can also manifest itself without involving any emotional suppression. For instance, let's say your partner unloads only their most powerful feelings and emotions regularly. Some people cannot hold back on certain beliefs, so they lash out. So, both of you end up feeling overwhelmed and confused, leading to another problem.

Experiencing these outbursts often enough, you can start feeling that it's your job to find a solution to your partner's issues. It's not enough to notice the anxiety and the strain it's putting on your relationship. You begin to get the feeling you are the sole savior of the relationship. Unfortunately, this usually worsens, as your partner could start developing resentment towards you for their behavior.

Another communication problem is when you consider expressing yourself as a risky affair. Maybe you are wondering what will happen if you reveal what you honestly think. It is enough to trigger your anxiety because you are afraid of the uncertainty of the outcome.

Frequently, this symptom stems from not having confidence in yourself, and you are worried about an adverse reaction from your partner. In this case, you might be taking a great deal of time to rehearse what you will say and complicate things further by imagining all the possible scenarios.

Mindful Communication

Mindful communication will help you learn some invaluable lessons. Here are a few:

Learn to Listen to Your Partner

Remember to be a good listener; this is something that your partner needs from you. Don't respond without actually listening to them and let them complete their sentences. Look in the eyes when they talk and show them that you are paying attention. Please pay attention to their words and their body language. Recognize what they are trying to convey to you. Listening well can help you know and understand your partner much better. Your partner will know that you care. Make them more comfortable around you. They will feel valued and will know that they can depend on you.

Learn to Be Non-Judgmental

You will learn how to be non-judgmental and provide a safe space for your partner to communicate with you. People are often afraid of conveying their true feelings or opinions when they think others will judge them. If you have a judgmental attitude, your partner will refrain from speaking honestly to you, as well. This means they don't feel comfortable with you and might look for this level of understanding from someone else. Be encouraging to your partner and let them know you respect their opinion, regardless of how different your own is.

View Problems More Objectively

People often react in the wrong way when their personal opinions or emotions cloud their judgment. Being objective is crucial if you want to resolve issues truly. If not, you will not be able to have a productive or honest conversation. This is important to foster growth and solve problems in your relationship. It would help if you kept your partner's perspective in mind before you reply to them. The more time you take to consider their view, the better you will solve the problem in an even-tempered way.

Control Your Life Better

Mindful communication, and mindfulness in general, can help you find more clarity in life. It will help you to avoid small problems that are often caused by bad communication. You will learn how to control your emotions and take control of how you handle different situations.

Mindfulness in Communication

Mindfulness will help you to understand your partner and maybe even learn from them. Your relationship will be strengthened, and you will make better choices for your overall benefit. Don't doubt the value of good communication skills.

When You Communicate With Your Partner

This will help you improve yourself as a person and increase personal growth. You will learn how to stabilize your relationship and take it in a positive direction, as well. Mindful communication can teach you how to control your thoughts, feelings, and actions in a positive way. Once you have this control, you can exercise it for your benefit. You will soon understand how some couples make it through thick and thin with the help of better communication.

Learning How to Listen to Your Partner

Good conversation is not just about what you're doing, but when you're doing it. We all know a conversation consists of two people who talk in exchange, sharing knowledge for mutual benefit and (hopefully) enjoyment. Unfortunately, in the hope of knowing them, too many of us are not listening to our conversation partner. We continue to listen only to know when we can take our place in the spotlight next time without being too rude! This means that two people may have what seems to be a conversation, but in fact, it is a simple game of "When do I get to talk next?" This kind of "conversation" is a total waste of time because no one gets the chance to know anything new, and there is no real relationship.

Many of us are bad listeners, but we fail to recall what other people tell us. Speaker and communications specialist Julian

Treasure states that we don't pay attention while we spend about 60 percent of our overall speaking time listening to other people. On average, we retain just 25 percent of what we hear. He claims that over the years, we have slowly lost our ability to listen at high quality. Why? In short, technology has made us lazy.

Since we've become accustomed to using copies of materials, books, images, and so on, we subconsciously assume that it doesn't matter if we're listening to it the first time because we can play it back or reread it later.

The Causes of Anxiety in a Relationship

Although anxiety comes from several different things, you need to understand how it happens to yourself individually, even a mixture of many things. You can learn about the fundamentals and have a clearer understanding of where these feelings begin. You should prevent these things by getting this experience easier and this insight to avoid being nervous again in the future.

The Root of the Problem

You must be able to recognize it before you work on fixing the problem. Although being critical of yourself is always a poor decision, in this situation, it becomes important. You have to understand what is causing them to deal with the difficulties you are having in your relationship. To see if you can get to the root of your dilemma, turn inward. Tell yourself why you want to conduct yourself the way you are. There will be no right or wrong response to this stage. No matter how you feel, you must have a justification for it, even if it is serious. Know that this may not be the healthiest choice, but it will become a restrained activity soon.

This will only be a waste of time and resources if you try to apply all the various fixes you know. Don't get upset because you don't see yourself or your relationship change. Take a more targeted plan. See if you can get to the very bottom of your concerns, understand them, and see them for what they are. Facing your issues in this way may be intimidating, but this is the way you're going to be able to resolve them. Know that you need to believe in yourself and that in the end, you need to trust. Problem-solving is hard for a cause, but the result will make you happy. The majority of them are bound to show up later when you just solve the surface layer. Getting down to the root of things makes sense.

Previous Relationships

If you have ever been in a relationship where you have been mistreated, you would naturally be wary about it in the future. For any abused person, it is a protective mechanism that is natural to take on. However, when you begin to put this position on your partner, it becomes a problem even when they are not abusive. Your persistent fear and judgment will ultimately lead your partner to many negative feelings, from vulnerability to rage. When you are not, it does not feel nice to be accused of being oppressive or manipulative.

Make sure that any questions you have about this problem are grounded in reality. If you have ever been broken up with or lied to, unexpected, cheated on, physically or mentally abused, then you are more likely to experience this kind of anxiety. It also has the power to shake you to your heart and alter you as a person when you are so seriously injured. Instead of comparing your current relationship to anything that might end up the same way, you must understand that you need to recover from the past.

Low Self-Esteem

This can show itself in many ways. Low self-esteem also comes with a lot of fear. You will find that you will start projecting your concerns, whether you are insecure about the way you look or your ability to impress your partner. If you feel disappointed in yourself, you will also begin to project this feeling and begin to believe that your partner is disappointed in you. Your partner has communicated this to you themselves; how to say if you are projecting or not is if their dissatisfaction has not been indicated, this feeling arises from your anxiety and begins being projected.

As you might imagine, it becomes very unreasonable when you start accusing your partner of feeling those ways when they say they don't. Fighting can become a rather stressful fight, one that sometimes proves it's not worth it. When you project emotions on your partner, you will know when they continually feel they have to prove to you how much they love you or how they see you. Reassurance is important in a relationship, but this can become stressful if they constantly convince you. It will probably not be enough to repair your low self-esteem, no matter what response you receive from them.

Not just your relationship. You need to focus on improving yourself. Understand that you are an individual with individual needs. In the mirror, you need to look at yourself and be satisfied with what you see and who you are. There will be a chance of projecting negative emotions on your partner if you feel anything less than this. Make sure you make self-care a priority. Understand that it is not selfish or excessive; for your mental health, it is necessary.

The Attachment Style

When you are a child, an attachment style is something that grows. You may either have a healthy sense of how to bond with others, depending on how you are raised, or you may feel like you constantly need to receive reassurance to know that you are cared for. As you reach maturity and get into serious relationships, this can probably end up being projected. Even if your parents made these choices, they would affect you for the rest of your life.

You might have established a habit of suppressing your feelings and needs if your parents were cold and withheld love. For long periods, babies left to cry learn how to self-soothe. This can be challenging because they are taught that no one will come for them when needed. You might feel this way about your wife, as translated into adulthood, or you might even believe that your feelings are not significant.

Having an anxious attachment means you're living in fear that at any moment, your partner will abandon you. During adolescence, these abandonment problems typically arise from watching a parent do the same thing. Children who come from broken homes will also learn to believe that not every person is permanent in their lives. You will never feel comfortable with your partner if you feel this way because you will always be waiting for them to leave you.

Loss of Trust

For several reasons, you may lose faith in your partner. It is the way you treat this feeling that will eventually decide whether it is an issue. Typically, if anyone loses their faith in another individual, they will have to prove themselves to be trustworthy again. If you are upset by their acts to forgive them or prefer to live your life by continually punishing them for what they have done, this is an indication that your guilt is driving you.

It could be likely that you have entered into a relationship with this mentality if you continuously experience a sense of dissatisfaction or negativity. It can be devastating not to have any confidence in your partner as the years go by. You are both going to believe like your efforts do not matter. You are going to grow a very apathetic attitude by always predicting the end of your relationship. This can serve as a defensive mechanism, but it is not the right way to deal with your confidence problems.

If you can work on these confidence issues and your partner, your relationship will stand a fighting chance. Are there concrete reasons you don't trust your partner anymore? You may have to turn your attention inward if you cannot think of factual explanations why your partner is untrustworthy. What makes you feel like this and why? It is important to get down to the deeper meaning behind the issue before responding to the surface problems. Enable yourself to examine these emotions and understand that they may derive from a skewed view of the relationship you've formed. Even if you want the relationship to last, it will be hard when your negativity cannot be set aside. These nervous thoughts will continually eat away at you, offering a diversion. This is not going to be fair to either one of you.

Misunderstanding

Fighting is natural in any safe relationship. Even though they are very close or have a good bond, couples do not get along 24/7. You are illustrating that you are still individuals by disagreeing. It's important to be able to stand up for what you believe in, even if you stand up against your partner. When two adults who love each other get into a confrontation, they should communicate through the problem. It doesn't indicate that the relationship is doomed, but that may also be what you are led to believe by your anxiety.

There are certain ways of war that can be risky. When rage becomes physical, this typically occurs. If you cannot talk about your emotions without getting too mad, this can lead to something bad. While you are trying to solve the original one, another bad sign is getting into additional disagreements. This may mean that there is a misunderstanding taking place. It can be difficult to get the right words out, but you should do so when talking to your partner. Correct them if they misinterpret you. Letting stuff make you even madder is not going to fix your problem.

The Tendency to Question

Do you ever overthink situations? Does it take long to make up your mind when you are offered a decision? As a partner, being this way means that you would also challenge your significant other to make your choices best. It's not necessarily bad to ask questions; getting these responses will provide you with clarification. When you are unable to trust or believe in your partner, this becomes harmful to your relationship. Your questions will start to sound accusatory, which may end up leading to defensive answers. It's an extremely frustrating problem to face telling the truth and not being believed, particularly coming from the person you expect to love and support you for who you are.

If you are an over-thinker, you will have the opportunity to easily construct multiple possibilities about what could be possible in your mind. Focusing on every aspect of your partner's conduct, for example, could lead you to an incorrect conclusion that they are dishonest with you. When you fall into this mindset and start telling yourself of things that are not supported by objective evidence, your actions would be labeled unhealthy. Realize that it is unreasonable to put these labels on your partner.

To fix this issue, you need to change your attention. Realize that your partner is a person with a different way of thinking. They say to you that the acts they chose to show should be the two modes of communication you should be holding onto. Try to let go of the what-ifs or the different scenarios that you build in your head. If your partner seems to be genuine with you, then you do not have to go on a search to find a reason why they may not be. Just because you are prone to looking at negative results does not mean that your partner will automatically fulfill them.

How to Overcome Anxiety in Relationship

Keep it real; relationships aren't easy; they take a lot of time. However, if you care and love the person for whom you are, the effort is worth it. All relationships will have challenges and problems that need to be paved (worked through) to a healthier relationship. It can vary depending on your relationship situation. Two people can solve these challenges and be a stronger couple.

Many people who care about each other tend to focus on problems rather than neglect them to expect that they are gone. By focusing together on these challenges, you create building blocks for a robust framework for your relationship. Yay, who's not going to want that? Understand that by keeping your feelings in check, conflicts won't be fixed, and challenges will continue to get worse in your relationship.

Trust

Many of us have confidence problems from past relationships that we always bring to our next relationships subconsciously. When you get into a mistrust relationship and can't let this suspicion go, how can your relationship progress?

By not believing that your partner comes from a position of love when they raise their doubts or issues about you and your relationship with you, you are typically not so open to listening. Know that your new relationship is not your history.

If obstacles arise and your partner can communicate these problems with you, trusting them does not mean you think you are a terrible person or want to isolate yourself until they tell you that you are horrible.

Hearing Your Partner

Many cats won't hear each other consciously. The second thing is negative; it can easily redirect, emotionally shut down, or get upset. Yikes! Yikes! It is not pleasant or constructive when your partner hears the awful stuff said and took away from the talk. Most people voice a problem because they want their partner to hear them and seriously say. Nobody wants to express and feel like they haven't been heard; it is hurtful and rude.

Give Constructive Feedback

We all need feedback, and not all input is sweet, warm, and smooth.

However, if you care for someone, be careful to give your name and to swear out your suggestions, as well as throw away things. Others can't listen if you're in mad assault mode.

Depending on the actual time you waited for that input or whether you spoke about that before and you did not see any changes in the situation, yes, there is probably a lot of anger and sternness in your speech, as well as a coherent delivery approach.

Be Open to Feedback

If you don't have suggestions, you can easily be identified as a "victim." If you want to address problems with someone and their first reaction is that they "can't do anything right," that's a flagrant cop-out. We'd love to believe our relationship is unsatisfactory and straightforward, but this is just dumb fantasy talk. Every relationship takes effort. If you think you will never do something right, most probably you will never.

Follow Through With Integrity

Having talked about the problem and thinking you're on the same page as your significant other (because they said you were) is a beautiful feeling, right? Well, if you think you're on the same page, it doesn't feel that good when then you find out that you aren't. Problems cannot be resolved if you are not open and honest about what is realistic and not. We do have our flaws and strengths. Sometimes we find partners in some of our characteristics that are opposite, which can be excellent. Nevertheless, if you don't want to work on issues openly, take advice from each other or find a habit that works for both of you.

Nobody wants to be with someone who only passively agrees in the hope that the problems magically disappear. It is a very untimely way not to deal with barriers that will exist. When we let go of the delusion that relationships are supposed to be perfect, easy to go, no arguments or struggles, we can successfully work on the severe problems that lift their ugly heads.

The overcoming of challenges starts with you. Don't make promises you can't fulfill. Never say that you're going to do something, and then you don't. Respect your partner and respect yourself more importantly by being frank.

Learn to Listen

Do you ever want to jump into the conversation while your partner still speaks? Or are you waiting in advance to ignore or even dismiss what your partner is trying to say in your two cents? One common complaint about couples is that "my partner doesn't listen to me." We tell our partner that it is essential to listen to understand and not prepare our discussion sides. By listening to knowledge without judgment, you assert, "I care about you and about what you think you are important to me."

- If you feel like cutting in, take a few deep breaths

- Make your partner's eye contact

- Carry a pen or clip for fidget management

- Describe what your partner said after your partner finishes talking

Avoid the Blame Game

If a dispute happens, the partner can easily be blamed. Instead of trying to find your partner's flaws, ask yourself if you contribute to the conflict. When couples sit together and take responsibility for their part, a sense of security and partnership is formed. It is much more connective and pro-resolution than being attacked and defended by so many couples. For example:

- How do you play the drama in the relationship?
- What is your capacity to make various choices?

If disagreements start to escalate, take a break. Calm down so that you can do it

Later, the dispute is relevant when cooler heads prevail. Processing means learning about how we can do it better next time without going back to the fight. A comment like "maybe I responded over" or "I should have done it better" does a great deal to reconnect and resolve disagreements. Know, a stable partnership takes two individuals to prioritize. Even though you cannot change your partner, you can check how you respond.

Making Time

We also spend less time with our partners and families in our busy lives than in other activities like work or entertainment. Are you doing your partner the best of your time? If not, this may be a significant challenge for the relationship if you have to insert it into your regular schedule yet ensure that you spend quality time together. Taking even 20 minors together with noisy telephones or TV creates a sense of "us." During these conversations, you can stop talking about relationship issues but you can face external stressors. It becomes a bonding ritual and describes the pair as a pair. Otherwise, you give your partner the signal that your interests lie elsewhere.

Do You Appreciate Each Other?

Failure to respect makes you feel unloved, inappropriate and misunderstood. When we show our respect and affection for our partner, we demonstrate what we love and admire. It is an opportunity to build on our partnership and friendship, the cornerstone of all relationships. Take the time to tell your partner when they do something you admire. "You have done this very well" or "You're so good with it." You both should do your best to thank each other for overcoming the barrier. For example:

- Do something extraordinary every day, like making coffee or writing a note

- Send a text message

- Cook a meal

- Give a small gift

- Say, "I love you"

You would be shocked how easy tasks are always done to improve your relationship.

Financial Issues

If you always meet to discuss who pays for dinner or a severe partnership to share the finances, money problems will impede your collaboration. Contact each other to keep things equal.

Discourse what money means to each one of you. When we learn the money symbolism for our partners, we can easily avoid falling into the trap.

Are You Having Fun?

What does it mean to be together if you don't want to do business with each other? Having laughter, laughing together, and doing enjoyable things contribute to improving the relationship with each other. Check your network for what's possible, and don't forget to do anything special for your partner!

Relationships are still a work in progress, and it should not be shocking to identify hurdles from time to time. However, if you notice that you always hit the brick wall after following these tips, it might be time for professional support.

Not Making Your Relationship a Priority

You shouldn't end your relationship with "I do" if you want to keep your love life going. "Relationships lose their brilliant luster," says Karen Sherman, author of *Marriage Magic!* Dig it, hold it, and finish it.

It is important to do the things you did when you were first dating:

- Show appreciation

- Complement each other

- Contact each other throughout the day

- Show interest individually

- Arrange date nights and time together just as like any other important event in your life

Have respect for each other. Say "I appreciate you" so that your partner knows that they matter.

Conflict

According to New York-based psychologist Susan Silverman, periodic conflict is a part of life. But it is time to break out of this unhealthy pattern if you and your partner feel like you are the star of the film *Groundhog Day's* nightmare edition—that the same scenario keeps repeating it day after day. When you make an effort, you will encounter your frustration and discuss the underlying problems calmly.

Silverman suggests that you and your partner should learn to disagree more civilly and helpfully. Include these tactics throughout who you are in this relationship. You don't know you're a victim. It is your option to respond. Be frank with yourself. If you are in the middle of an argument, do your remarks center on conflict resolution, or are you asking for a reimbursement? It is best to take a deep breath and change your approach if your comments are accusing and hurtful.

Turn it up. Change it up. If you continue to react in the way that pain and unhappiness have taken you in the past, this time, you can't expect another outcome. Just a slight change will make a huge difference. If you usually leap right in before your partner finishes speaking, pause for a few moments. You'll be shocked how such a slight tempo shift can change the entire tone of an argument.

Offer something; get a lot. Offer a little. Excuse yourself when you're wrong.
Indeed, it's hard, but try to see a marvelous thing happen.

Relationship Conflicts

Conflicts in relationships are inevitable. It could arise from career, financial problems, your families who try to be a part of your relationship decisions, children's education, and others. All of these elements, along with some more, are the primary source of arguments that tend to take place between partners. The ultimate result of all this is nothing but relationship conflict.

Whenever anything of this sort tends to happen, do not worry much. It has been found that fights and arguments in relationships might bring out something good in relationships. However, it does not mean that you will permit negative events or situations to last for a long time.

You will have to manage all such situations properly to find serenity, complicity, and, above all, to reignite the flame of the relationship. To ensure that the relationship can resume or continue with a great start, you cannot ever permit things to worsen. You will only be harming the state of your relationship if you decide to sit idle, thinking everything will be fine the following day. If you ever fail to respond timely and allow the conflict to be as it is in the relationship, you will only be risking your relationship to the verge of separation.

Reasons behind Relationship Conflicts

To face the biggest monster in your relationship, along with the fears, you will have to start by learning the origin of conflicts in your relationship. Until you can figure out the point of origin, you will never get the chance to resolve the same. It is essential to place your finger right on the point of origin. To solve a problem properly, you will have to learn about the roots. Otherwise, you will end up applying a band-aid on the deep wounds. Even minimal tensions can slowly transform into a big fight if you have the habit of keeping your issues in the relationship unresolved. So, the very first step in getting rid of relationship conflicts is to recognize them properly.

Conflicts Arising From Professional Life

Tensions in the relationship are bound to arise when you try to give more importance to your professional career than your relationship and partner. The same works for the other person, as well. A situation of this nature might force either of the partners to react harshly. Nothing in this world can feel worse than the feeling of being left alone or abandoned by your partner. Trying to concentrate more on your professional life is unhealthy for you while being in a relationship. It can have some very serious effects on your family life as well. It might even be hard for you to reconcile work and family at times, especially when trying to start something new in your professional life. But for maintaining a proper balance in your life and staying away from all forms of relationship conflicts, you will need to learn the steps required to disconnect yourself from the world of your work. You will have to dedicate a proper time to enjoy your life with all those who matter to you.

Infidelity and Improper Behavior

You will have to ground certain attitudes as you become a part of a serious relationship. If you try to stick to some behavior that is not considered forgivable by your partner, you might find it tough to gather the broken pieces. You will be unknowingly forcing your relationship in the direction of some serious turbulence. Also, there might be some serious conflicts between you and your partner if there is a presence of infidelity.

Failure to Meet Expectations

Our lives are bound to grow, evolve, and change. Our relationships in life also pass through these three stages.

Sometimes, both the partners in a healthy relationship tend to develop separately. They arrive at a point where they are no longer the people they used to be during the initial phase of the relationship. Whenever anything happens, sit down with your partner and talk about the relationship. What are the expectations that both of you have? What are the expectations that are not being met? Are the expectations even reasonable? The perfect way of determining the position and condition of your relationship is by discussing the same.

To overcome all sorts of conflicts in your relationship, no matter the point of origin, you will need to start understanding why the conflicts even exist. To achieve this successfully, try to have some meaningful discussion with your partner. The conversation might not seem to be very comfortable for both of you. However, it is necessary for the betterment of the relationship. You will notice that your level of anxiety is getting heightened. But make sure that you do not let them push you in the direction of rude and harsh behaviors. Calm and controlled discussions can effectively help you deal with fights and conflicts instead of anxiety-filled arguments. No one loves to deal with conflicts. The primary reason behind this is to stay away from all forms of tension in the relationship. Some couples have the habit of blaming one another for arguments. Reactions of this sort can never resolve struggles. They will exacerbate all the issues.

Struggles are bound to come in life and relationships. The moment you try to ignore them, they will start harming you. When you challenge them face-toface, you will get the chance to turn them into useful tools to help you and your partner resolve the conflicts. You will get the opportunity to develop in the relationship, hand in hand. Also, struggles might creep in from several wrong assumptions about:

- The nature of the relationship

- Work and job

- How certain things are needed to be done in and around the house

- Varying obligations of the partners

- Wide differences in wants, needs, morals, or values

- Bad communication

Dealing with Conflicts

If you have ever been in a genuine and healthy relationship, you will be aware that disagreements and fights are nearly inevitable. When two people decide to share most of their time, having their lives and interests intertwined, no other person can stop them from disagreeing.

Disagreements in relationships can be big or small. For example, whether one of the partners should move to a new place for the other's career, decide about children's upbringing, or cook for dinner. But the fact is that quarreling or fighting with your partner is not the real trouble in your relationship.

If you can handle them perfectly, your conflicts can serve as a tool for enhancing the chore of your relationship. When two partners never discuss their issues or problems and keep fighting over something, meeting a common ground will be hard. When you decide to deal with your conflicts in a relationship in a constructive way, you will get the chance to understand your partner better.

Conflict of any kind with your romantic partner can make you feel attacked, weak, threatened, and vulnerable. It might even make you recoil and retreat. If you decide to opt for a silent treatment every time you feel offended or let down by your partner, it will be hampering the relationship instead of doing anything good. The result will be the breaking up of your relationship. The path or way that you and your partner choose to resolve conflicts can help determine whether your relationship is healthy or not.

Focus Examination

Any conflict can take the shape of something harmful when you try to focus on being defensive rather than problem resolution. By focusing only on your pain and suffering, you will be making sure that you experience all of them for the rest of your life. It is primarily because of the spot where you try to focus. Your flow of energy will be in that direction only. Your focus helps in determining the life directions. If you do not want to hit the wall, you will have to focus on all those things you desire—to be on the road. When you can alter your focus, you will be able to change the results of your life as well.

When you try to pay all your attention to where you do not desire the relationship to go, do not let anger develop or fight. You will only end up either in a painful or unsatisfied relationship or just separated from your partner. As you decide to work as a team to resolve the conflicts, you can easily attain those desired outcomes.

Shaping Conflicts into Opportunities

Do not try to win, do not get defensive, and do not keep pestering on a single point. Why would someone desire to lose that person whom they love? When you can properly understand that no one loses in the game of love, you will be able to shift all your attention from small arguments. You will be able to develop healthy communication in this way.

Conflicts are nothing but opportunities in disguise. They can act as a chance for every conflicting partner to align their outcomes and beliefs properly. They can be an opportunity of embracing, appreciating, and understanding the existing differences. Whenever you find yourself thinking only about your good, try to stand in the shoes of your partner. Try your best to get their point of view. However, constantly trying to opt for comfort will never allow you to grow.

Use of Humor

If you find yourself and the relationship in a dangerous cycle, a perfect way of breaking the pattern is to start using humor. Humor has always been regarded as very effective in relieving tension. It will allow your partner and you to focus on all those aspects that both of you desire and want. Learning several ways to save your relationship is always a better thing than arguing on what both the partners do not like, thus resulting in another argument.

If you feel that an argument is slowly escalating, take your time to focus on derailing the same. Give your best for arguing with a humorous tone. You can also opt for singing something funny as you argue that can make your partner laugh. The target is to make the conflict look ridiculous. As you both smile and laugh together, you will be able to strengthen the base of your relationship.

Nurturing Acceptance

We are not perfect. Our partners tend to do certain things or have certain habits that can annoy us at times. Instead of thinking of your partner's bad habits or negative traits, try to shift your focus on all those things they can present on the table. Concentrate on the qualities of your partner that you love and how they make you feel. You will notice that you can now easily change the direction of your mind from all those silly things that made you angry or go mad at your partner.

Just keep one thing in mind—it is about a person who you truly love and adore. You are not required to think of the negative traits as the prime qualities of your partner. You will have to put in some energy to understand the negative traits and flaws of one another. Both of you act like the supporting pillars of your lovely relationship. You will have to support your partner whenever necessary and vice versa.

Relationship between Anxiety and Conflicts

hen issues start cropping up in your relationship, you might have the W feeling that your anxieties are being warranted. You might start feeling that all your worries are coming to be true. Try your best not to get indulged in thoughts of this type. Anxiety generally originates from the unknown. Conflicts tend to arise whenever the expectations or needs are not met or differences in opinions. They might turn out to be healthy if handled in the right way, while anxieties are nothing but harmful. Some of the definite ways in which conflicts can affect anxiety are:

Increased Heartbeat

Conflicts result in the release of adrenaline. It can be made worse by anxiety. It might result in a rapid heartbeat, which can slowly escalate to shortness of breath. Conflict, coupled with anxiety, can make these physiological symptoms bad. It takes the structure of a vicious cycle. The best way of combating this is by approaching conflict face to face with calmness. If you can try to avoid being upset, raise your voice, or react in anger, you can easily prevent the trigger of an adrenaline rush. It can successfully suppress anxiety feelings.

Nervous Movement or Energy

Again, an adrenaline rush comes into play. You will feel your body suddenly getting filled with excessive energy that needs to be used somehow. As at the time of an argument, you are most likely not to fight or run, the energy gets transformed into pacing, hand wringing, toe-tapping, along specific other nervous movements. All these might turn out to be very disturbing for your partner and also yourself when you are in the mid-way of a conflict. Indeed, the fault is not yours. But the knowledge of the same will not make it fade away. All you can do is face the situation with a calm mind to prevent the adrenaline rush.

Anxiety and Panic Attacks

Anxiety can effectively lead to panic and anxiety attacks, which is nothing new. But you need to remember that while conflicts occur, it is for your good that you keep calm if you have problems with panic and anxiety. Such situations can easily trigger an attack, which can make everything go worse. Anxiety and panic attacks are generally characterized by:

- Sweating

- Difficulty breathing

- Difficulty concentrating

- A feeling of unknown doom

- Racing thoughts

Although there is nothing new to say, these symptoms are not funny. So, you need to be mindful before getting into an argument that you might face an attack if you fail to be level-headed.

Being Defensive

Nothing can be more destructive to the constructive resolution of conflicts than the habit of defensiveness. Anxiety can effectively block out the rational portion of your mind that plays the part of thinking about a situation with logic. When this logic is not present, you might face a tough time focusing on your partner's being said. You are most likely to shift your focus from listening to lashing out.

You will turn out the defensive shield, even in situations when your partner is not attacking you. You should defend your position when you are being treated unjustly. However, if your partner is willing to opt for a peaceful resolution, the best action is to match their intentions. You will need to drop your defensive shield for the betterment of the relationship. But when you are having anxious thoughts, doing all these is not going to be easy.

Shut Down

In place of just turning on your defensive mode, you might choose to shut down completely. Your anxious mind might find it tough to process all those things that are happening. The lack of energy during the situation can lead to a complete shutdown. As such a thing happens, you will not be able to concentrate or focus. You will not be able to call out rationality or logic for working through the conflict.

Also, you will not be able to comprehend what is being said by your partner. You will be feeling empty and heavy on the inside, feeling like a battery that has drained suddenly. The best thing that can be done on your side in such a situation is relaxing and mending. Conflicts will be in place unless you can take back control over your mind and activate rationality.

How to Successfully Overcome a Bad Relationship Dispute

When you face a conflict in your healthy and growing relationship, try to think about how you can talk or express your feelings regarding this conflict. The primary aim is to establish a good communication model. Good communication is where every individual can check the stock and get an idea about the other person's attitude. Conflict resolution will seem a lot easier to manage when it is not escalated with unnecessary things such as angry tones. For effective communication during conflicts, you will need to follow three simple rules:

- Keep your calm, and do not raise your voice

- Let your partner talk. Let them develop the state of the argument, as communication not only includes talking but also listening

- However, try to reach a middle ground, but do not opt for compromises that can negatively affect the coming days

A couple who has the habit of arguing and respects all these rules can quickly resolve.

Required Actions for Overcoming Conflicts between Partners

Relationships are not meant to be easy. You will keep learning when you are in a healthy relationship. Is it even possible to not repeat the mistakes and stabilize the base of your romantic relationship? Is it possible to manage the relationship conflicts without you being hurt? Try to follow all these recommendations for rebuilding the love in your struggling relationship.

After you are well aware of the reasons behind the relationship tensions that tend to shake the relationship base, you can focus on moving to a more "direct" phase of harmony. Yes, the first phase might turn out to be very psychological as you will need to communicate with the other person. However, it is necessary if you want to bring back your relationship on its track.

It is essential to use more thoughtful and technical actions to find your partner's heart. It is also needed to overcome the relationship crisis. The actions that you decide to use need to correspond with various issues. Otherwise, your actions will not have any effect on the situation. It can even aggravate the issues. Do not just opt for resolution for the sake of being done with it; opt for a solution for making the situation better.

Do not keep assigning blame to the other side. A relationship is not a oneperson game. It is all about team effort. Both partners are required to be in the relationship altogether. If one of the partners keeps on giving effort while the other sits idle, it will be better for the relationship to exist.

If you and your partner are not feeling satisfied or fulfilled in your relationship, you must spend more time together. It will help you both to understand the problems in a better way. You will also come to know what you both want and need from the relationship.

Every relationship in this world is bound to go through conflicts at some point or the other. All that is important for you to know is that disagreements are not always a bad thing. It is how individuals in relationships try to express their varying views on a topic or situation.

Compromising as a Common Solution

The use of compromise in relationships is widespread for resolving disputes and disagreements in the mediation and negotiation process. While it can lead to an agreement's production, compromise is not powerful enough for resolving conflicts all the time. It cannot work specifically in situations when there are some underlying organizational or interpersonal conflicts.

The prime reason for this is that compromise is a settled resolution to an issue. It is not at all the ultimate solution that is sought by either partner. It can effectively generate material or a functional solution, but it cannot resolve behavioral or emotional issues that are coupled with disagreements. As a result, either one of the partners or both will continue to carry forward certain ill feelings or dissatisfaction that might come to the surface once again if the issue arises.

Compromise is defined as a win/lose agreement where both partners tend to get something they wish for, but it is not possible to attain everything that they want. The majority of the tensions or issues crop up with a collaborative or competitive strategy. The outcome that is best possible in such a situation is the ultimate goal of both partners. But various other vital factors come into the equation, such as financial cost, time requirement, practical matters, and use of power. The ultimate realization that the desired outcomes might turn out to be unachievable can force the partners to negotiate. It involves the concept of giving and take for reaching a mutual agreement of compromised nature.

Agreeing to Disagree

Using a compromise for settling a dispute or conflict requires both partners to know that the result might be less than they hoped for. The ultimate decision might be the one that is acceptable. However, not optimal. You may feel resistance or reluctance to compromise to resolve conflicts when you think the result will be lost. When the primary focus is on things that are achieved instead of things that have been given up, chances of acceptance and satisfaction of both partners are high. Compromise will turn out to be a successful venture if both partners have a choice of tangible outcomes. The outcomes are required to be open for consideration so that the final decision remains within a standard box for both partners.

There might be a requirement to "agree to disagree" at some point when the issues seem incurable, and the realization that they will be unable to agree to sets in. Agreeing to disagree is essential when the disagreement is over principles or values rather than methods or facts. When both partners can learn to listen to each other and respectfully understand the other person's point, accepting the disagreements will seem a lot easier. A mutual form of acceptance regarding the differences can improve the likelihood of a proper resolution to any issue or dispute.

Compromise can turn out to be a perfect and effective method for resolving differences and conflicts. However, it can't be the right choice all the time. Even when other modes of conflict seem more appropriate, opting for compromise can lead to an outcome that is of no use for the current situation. You will need to make sure that essential requirements or vital issues are not lost during compromise. Sometimes you might need to opt for other creative solutions. All forms of disagreements and differences are not needed to be negotiated.

Stop Negative Thinking

If the glass is half empty, it is almost difficult in each encounter to see the positive, potential, or silver linings and life lessons. It is challenging for you or your partner to be content with this mindset in a partnership. If your partner feels they cannot please you and maximize your satisfaction, they can feel less, weak, inadequate, etc.

Rewire your brain. Recognize and transform a negative thought or belief into one of the most positive thoughts you have developed. This is an unbelievably significant change in your mind, so it takes time, energy, and persistence to get the idea you want in a safer, new way. However, once you constantly correct it, you will see that your negative thoughts dissipate, and healthier ones arise. This is how you take down the negative lens and look at the world more honestly and with more hope.

Below are a few other tips to make your dating and relationship life more satisfying as you change your mind to achieve the love you wish for.

- Always remember that taking care of your expectations is important to your relationship's success. Discrepancies and conflicts are inevitable in the world of relations, so remember that it is natural and all right. The most important thing is how you and your partner manage and develop in difficult times.

- Remember, your partner is also a person. Not all your partner does is "right" or "good," but you resist the urge to change your critical lens when you are frustrated. Communicate your desires, and do not try to generalize the entire relationship for a moment when you feel hurt.

- Consider the partner deliberately in a positive light. Thank your partner for the little things and compassion that they show. Say thank you. It perpetuates a cycle of optimistic and caring relationships.

- Do not take things personally. There will be poor dates, difficult conversations, and times that can be frustrating. Do not add these experiences to your negative pile. Take life lessons instead and imagine yourself moving towards your goals. Engage yourself to be happy on your journey to marriage.

How to Overcome Negative Thinking

There are several kinds of things that can ruin an entirely good relationship. Cheating and incompatibility, for example, are two major issues. There is one thing that can, more than anything else, ruin a relationship, according to experts.

"The biggest killer of the relationship can be negative thoughts," says Bustle licensed psychologist Nicole Issa, Psy. D. "There is a very close feedback link between the emotions, feelings, and actions. Having negative thoughts will take you down the rabbit hole." It is important to know from Dr. Issa that your thinking habits will contribute to important problems with your relationships. For example, early childhood encounters with your parents can make you feel unworthy of love. That is why you may get into all relationships believing that your partner is about to abandon you at some stage, and you may be afraid to speak up.

"The truth is that we are making our own reality," Joann Cohen, matchmaker and dating coach, says to Bustle. "If we believe we have a good relationship, we work through things that we are always ok. But when you come to relationships with a negative thought, you always expect the worst not only for your partner but also for the outcome of your relationship." It is essential for you to find ways to make them positive in order to prevent negative thoughts. According to experts, listed below are some things you can do to stop toxic ideas, sabotaging your relationship.

The First Time You Have Fallen in Love with Your Partner

When you pass a rough patch, it is easy to let that cloud judge you. Talk about your partner's "real" feelings when you start invading your mind the first time you fell in love with them and talk about how you felt. "Shutting your eyes and seeing the bright eye person with whom you fell in love will make things look much more positive and doable," says Cohen. At times, we need only a little reminder of the good times to resolve the poor.

Let Go of the Past

Giving up the past is easier said than done. "We all have a piece of our history with us to 'shield' us against getting hurt again," says Cohen. "And if you continue to bring your old relations and harm to your new relationship, then you sabotage and create the truth that things just do not or will not work." Then, try to separate your past from your present to prevent your past from creating toxic thoughts. No matter how much they look, speak, or behave the same, your ex is not your current partner.

If you can separate your relationship from your new one, being more involved is easier for you.

Find Other Ways to Express Your Energy

Toxic thinking will cause you to do unreasonable, relationship-sabotage stuff like hack into your partner's phone. To counter this phenomenon, Dr. Issa says that she knows what your thoughts are doing. For instance, why do you feel you need to just "check" in your partner 20 times in a row? You would also want some affirmation or confirmation that your partner cares. "Once you know that you can do (these) stuff, take some time to practice those skills to help you like to count to ten and relax," she says. Find ways to reduce the intense feelings you have to not act in ways that you will regret.

Do Not Conclude You Know What Your Partner Is Thinking

Negative thoughts are often based on perceptions that do not always exist. "If we put our negative feelings on somebody else or place them on your significant other, the anger of the other person is what you are reading," Cohen says. The important thing here is never to presume. Do not jump to conclusions. Do not cook it yourself if you cannot help it. Get to the edge and chat with your friend. "Try or ask for clarification. Take the words on face value," she says. "You never believe you know how they feel."

Have That One Person You go-to to Vent Your Anger

If you are mad about your partner, it is not uncommon to put all your problems to anyone who is listening. Suppose you are mad about your partner, but, according to Cohen, "When you do that, you create a gap between your meaningful other person and your world, creating more negativity than you know." If you must lower yourself down, choose one person, and stay with them. "Saying to everyone is not helpful to your ugly business and will only encourage more negative feelings," she says.

Create a List of Your Toxic Thoughts

Preventing toxic thoughts from destruction takes some self-reflection with constructive alternatives. Take a move and make a hard proof for or against any thought. After that, come up with a more concise and adaptive alternative thinking. For example, if you think your partner is no longer interested in you because they did not reply to your text, please list all other things they could do. "Think about other occasions they have taken a while to answer or to show that they are still involved," says Dr. Issa. "Here the alternative thought maybe as simple as just an 'I have not heard of them, yet it does not mean they do not care.'" Then, the more detailed you are, the more effective it will be.

Take Breaking-Up Totally Off the Table

Whatever the toxic thoughts are, usually, they are from the same location— fear. In particular, the fear that your partner will leave. "I use the analogy, 'you'll burn the ship' when you comment," Cohen says. "There is no other way to get out of the island when you burn the ship, so work together to survive." If there is no solution, you start seeing what is good in a situation. When you take the chance to break the equation (that is, "burning the ship"), you can support your relationship from a place of love and not fear. If your words and actions come from a place of affection, it is much easier for you to remain positive.

Thinking is only a thought at the end of the day. It is not necessarily the truth. If you do not let your relationship consume you, it will improve your relationship.

Importance of Working on Yourself

Sometimes it appears to be simpler to adore others than to cherish yourself. However, self-acknowledgment is an essential piece of building solid associations with others. Luckily, with a little arrangement and development, you can likewise figure out how to cherish yourself.

Forgive Yourself Not Matter Your Past

A common obstacle to self-love is that all of us used to have things we could not forgive. Maybe we feel sad about how we treat our ex. Or we think that we are too short with our family because of depression or fatigue. Or maybe we have experienced months/years of losing streaks in our lives, which is not unforgivable.

Here are some things to do to forgive yourself:

Focus on Your Feelings

One of the first steps to understand how to forgive yourself is to focus on your feelings. You need to identify and process the emotions before you can move on. Give yourself permission to understand and acknowledge the feelings you have caused and embrace them.

Acknowledge Your Error Out Loudly

When you make a mistake and keep struggling to let it go, acknowledge what you've learned from the error. When you speak out the thoughts in your mind and your heart's feelings, you can be free from any of the pressures. You also cement on your memory what you have learned from your acts and consequences.

Discuss With the Own Critic

Journaling will help you consider your internal criticism and improve selfcompassion. Pickell says one thing you should do is write a "conversation" with you and your inner critic. This will help you see patterns of thinking that sabotage your capacity to forgive yourself.

You should also use your diary to make a list of the things you enjoy about yourself, including your strengths and talents. This will help boost your selfconfidence when you believe you have made a mistake.

Show Goodness and Compassion to Yourself

If your first reaction to a negative situation is to blame yourself, it's time to demonstrate some kindness and consideration. The best way to continue the path of forgiveness is to be loving and compassionate towards yourself. This takes effort, maturity, and a reminder to your person that you deserve forgiveness.

Spend Time with Yourself Alone

Whether you're unmarried, in a romantic relationship, or married, one of the easiest ways to maintain a loving relationship with yourself is to spend time alone daily. Irrespective of your introvert or extrovert status, everybody will benefit from some real-time alone.

Take Yourself to an Eatery

Go by yourself to a movie. I am taking a long morning stroll. Rest on your bed and take a deep breath. Meditate for a couple of minutes in the evening. Whatever activity alone draws you to time, make it happen. When you allow yourself the time and room to listen to yourself, you might be surprised by what ideas and revelations pop up for you.

Make Sure You Insert Play into Your Daily Activities

The re-prioritization of play into your life is one of the most significant improvements. Sat down with yourself and demanded, "What did I do before life got so serious for fun?" and then began to honor the responses that came to you.

After this discovery, you begin to take improve lessons, take more pictures, make more short videos, and dancing. If your very meaningful, very frustrating adult life has taken a backseat to play, you will need to reprioritize some stuff.

Restrict the Quantity of Junk Food That Your Brain Consumes

Just like your body gets grumpy if you regularly feed it awful stuff, so does your disposition when you provide junk to your mind.

Avoid watching the news. There's a fair possibility that the bulk of the information delivered to you is pointless, and fear-based, depending somewhat on which country you live in. Avoid eating such garbage to the best of your ability. Instead, consume only highly enriching information.

Unfollow or unfriendly people who perpetuate hate and negativity through the social network newsfeed. I've got about four thousand Facebook contacts. Still, I only subscribe to less than 40 of them. Just as you carefully examine the kind of food you ingest, you must be extra careful concerning the type of information, news, or gossip you expose yourself to. Both of them matter more than you feel they do.

Sleep Adequately Well

Approximately a third of your time is spent on the bed sleeping, so you may as well be skillful at it. We may be deprived and exhausted by the way we sleep, or it can invigorate and elevate us.

Get some good quality blackout curtains, restrict some electronic light emission within 2 hours of going to sleep, and keep your bedroom free from any mobile phones/laptops/TVs. It's time to cuddle or have sex when the lights go out, not update your Instagram feed.

Specific Things as Your Targets and Be Intentional

In your life, impose real restrictions such that you take time for the items that matter most to you. Say no to people with whom you do not want to share time. Say no to tasks at work that do not serve you and your core beliefs. Spend time daily among your favorite pals. In your year, take out time and allow time for laughter, lightness, and playfulness.

With how you invest your time, the more you honor yourself, the more your inner child can feel heard, understood, and cherished.

Create Time for Relaxation

You want to make sure you still give yourself the freedom and room to breathe and enjoy amongst all of your nutritious foods, optimized sleep patterns, and playfulness.

When you feel like it, take naps. When you like them, treat yourself to spa services. Let yourself soak in the salt baths of Epsom for an hour while you are in the mood. In the self-care/self-love journey, rest is crucial. Allow yourself to have no plans occasionally.

Often, having a rest, laying down on the concrete, and just breathing is the only thing you can do for yourself.

Keep Your Boundaries

Write a list of the things you emotionally need, things that are important to you, and whether they are neglected or violated, annoy you or hurt your feelings. They may include being listened to; getting sympathy when you are broken; being celebrated when you succeed; receiving affection and tenderness without asking for it; being looked after and understanding that everyone will be relying on you. For you, whatever is essential. And when someone violates what's valuable to you or crosses your lines, when it hurts, you will know. Don't disregard that. Some thoughts tell you what is right and what is wrong.

Let everyone around you know what the limits are and what you will accept and what you will not allow. You can excuse them if they apologize. You ought to establish consequences if they do not or continue to ignore the boundaries and desires. If you talk to your partner that you need them to hear you and understand your emotions and they continually ignore you or advises you to get over it, you should proceed with suitable action, such as seeking somebody else to trust.

Do Care for Yourself as Well as You Do for Anyone

It looks easy, but many of us don't do this because we think we're greedy or that it's not necessary to have our own needs met. No, to think about yourself is not selfish. Compassion for oneself implies expressing empathy for your own and other emotions. With gentleness, concern, and consideration, handle yourself how you would take your kids or your closest mate.

Surprise Yourself

Discover stuff out of your reach to say yes to, stuff that you usually wouldn't say yes to. It would also help you get to understand yourself as well. You may discover that you like things that you have never seen or attempted before. Try and move away from your comfort zone to see what will happen (it's most definitely going to be positive!).

Find Something You Love Doing

It's convenient when you're feeling down about yourself to get caught in a rut. Whether it's golfing, gardening, cooking, picking an activity, sport, or art that you love.

Discover anything that you love to do—anything. "The likelihood is that if you enjoy doing it, then you're pretty good at it, too," says Jamie Katoff, LMT, a San Francisco-based marital therapist. "When we're doing things we enjoy (and doing it well), we go through a condition called 'flow,' which increases feelings of trust and overall satisfaction." Learning how to be more consistent in that condition can contribute to more vital self-love and self-esteem feelings.

Conclusion

A relationship is meant to bring people joy, not agony. By focusing on your mental health first, you'll be much better equipped to help your loved one as well. The biggest tip for coping with anxiety in a relationship is to keep the lines of communication open. Just because your partner may not be struggling with a disorder like anxiety doesn't mean they won't need you on their side during trying times.

When your partner needs help, and you're too afraid or too busy to provide it, your relationship will inevitably suffer. Even small things like having a meal together once a week can make a huge difference in the health of your relationship. Being committed to working together and being honest about your feelings can help you overcome any obstacles that may arise.

It's okay to feel nervous about your partner. If you're having doubts about the relationship, it's okay to ask for some space until you can work through your feelings. Just know that if you're able, it takes a lot of energy and courage and probably a bit of self-reflection as well. If there are any signs your partner is struggling with anxiety, don't ignore them.

Even if you feel like the anxiety is insurmountable, or the relationship is over, remember that there are always options such as therapy. It takes two to work a relationship, and even though recovery from anxiety can take time and effort, it's worth it in the long run.

Treating an anxiety disorder can often be difficult, but it can positively impact your life and those around you. It's important to remember that everyone will have their days when they are struggling with anxiety. The important thing is to talk about these struggles, seek support, and most importantly, stay connected with your partner.

Hopefully, this helps you find the right path to finding happiness in your relationship and feel a little bit more prepared for the future. If you're going through some anxiety in your relationship, try not to be too hard on yourself. If something is complicated or if it seems like you're getting nowhere, then consider hiring a therapist to help you overcome the problems that may be along the way. If you've just gotten out of a toxic relationship and are trying to find someone to spend your time

with and love, then consider seeking more counseling

www.ingramcontent.com/pod-product-compliance
Lightning Source LLC
LaVergne TN
LVHW051304200726
843510LV00010B/1270